The Nobel Prize Acceptance Speech: New and Selected Wayman Poems

Tom Wayman

Cover design and illustrations by William Johnson
Photos by Judy Wapp
Sculpture by Jon Taylor, *Frog Poetry Reading* 1978

Published Fall 1981 by

Thistledown Press
668 East Place
Saskatoon, Sask.
S7J 2Z5

Canadian Cataloguing in Publication Data

Wayman, Tom, 1945 -
    The Nobel Prize Acceptance Speech

        Poems
        ISBN 0-920066-46-1 (bound)
        ISBN 0-920066-45-3 (paperback)

        I. Title
        PS 8595.A93N6   C811'54   C81-091209-0
        PR 9199.3.W39N6

ACKNOWLEDGEMENTS

"On Relating California Atrocity Tales," "Poem Composed In Rogue River Park, etc.", "Flying", "Life On The *Land Grant Review*", "Influences", "Waiting For Wayman", "Wayman In Love", "Getting Fired", "Wayman In The Workforce: Urban Renewal" from *Waiting For Wayman,* and "Metric Conversion", "Travelling Companions" from *Living On The Ground: Tom Wayman Country* are reprinted by permission of The Canadian Publishers, McClelland and Stewart Limited, Toronto. "The Day After Wayman Got The Nobel Prize", "Wayman In The Workforce: Teacher's Aide," "Dead End", from *For And Against The Moon,* "Becoming A Crank", "Wayman In Circulation", "Not Getting Hired", "Wayman In The Workforce: Actively Seeking Employment", "The Kenworth Farewell" from *Money And Rain,* and "Wayman In Quebec", "Wayman Ascending Into The Middle Class" from *Free Time* were published by The Macmillan Company of Canada Limited and are reprinted by permission of Gage Publishing Limited. "Transport" was first published in *The Paris Review* and subsequently as a broadside by the Dreadnaught Press, Toronto; "Receding" appeared in *The Ontario Review;* "Wayman On Air", "Wayman On Air: 2. Interviewing", and "Wayman On Air: 3. Editing" were published in *Saturday Night;* "The Detroit State Poems: Security" was published in *The Little Magazine* and "Meeting Needs" appeared in *The Fiddlehead.*

This book has been published with the assistance of the Saskatchewan Arts Board and The Canada Council.

TABLE OF CONTENTS

for Glen Sorestad

WHAT AM I DOING HERE?

"The university where I went to study writing in the late 1960s is in the very heart of southern California, about fifteen miles from Anaheim, where Disneyland is. One of the great things about living down there was the chance it gave me to drive north to visit Vancouver again and tell all sorts of lies about the things I had heard, seen, or even participated in . . ."

On Relating California Atrocity Tales

Their eyes glaze, and thin tongues
slip out to moisten lips.
Faces peer into an imagined sunshine
and palm trees. "Tell us again.
At the height of a party, you coat yourselves
in Mazola oil, lie in a pile, and at a signal
writhe? You have seen clinches between
young men and 50-year-old housewives?
The very rugs steam
at the whispers of the golden sexless
surfers? Men with bleached hair?
Jill marrying John because,
because he has a *truck*?"

The words cackle in their minds.
And long after Wayman has suavely bowed
and dropped South again,
they remember. They remember.
Huddled as close to the border as they can,
they feel a heat drifting up
past Oregon and Washington. They write:
"You said that people there say
California is at most a year ahead?"
They shift uneasily in their chairs,
rubbing their hands together in the cold;
and slowly turn their palms out,
one by one, toward what they hope is Anaheim.

11

"Driving back and forth between Vancouver and California, which I have continued to do ever since, has led to many unpleasant incidents involving my car. The next poem is about one such occurrence . . ."

Poem Composed In Rogue River Park, Grants Pass, Oregon After Wayman's Car Stopped Dead On The Oregon Coast In The Middle Of A Howling Rainstorm And Had To Be Towed First To Yachats, Oregon, Where It Couldn't Be Fixed And Then One Hundred Miles Through The Mountains To Eugene, Where After It Was Repaired And Wayman Started Out Again His Accelerator Cable Parted And He Had To Run On The Last Dozen Miles Or So Into Grants Pass At Midnight With His Throttle Jammed Open And Spend The Night Waiting For The Garage To Open Which Is At This Moment Working On His Car, Or Rather Waiting For A New Part To Be Shipped Down From Eugene (And Which Garage, Incidentally, Would Fix The Cable But Fail To Discover That All That High-Rev Running Would Have Blown The Head Gasket On Wayman's Car Causing Frightening Over-Heating Problems The Next Day When Wayman Did Try To Blast On Down To San Francisco)

Let me not go anywhere.
Let me stay in Grants Pass, Oregon, forever.

"Every form of travel has its own unpleasantnesses, though. One method of getting from place to place I'm not particularly fond of is flying . . ."

Flying

Tonight look up when a plane passes:
Wayman may be aboard.
Sealed in a cabin miles above
sweet wars and friendly auto wrecks
Wayman pulls his seatbelt tighter and tighter

and listens.
He waits for the change in the engines
that will herald the sickening spin.
He waits for the whisper of the other, colliding craft,
for the tick of the time bomb . . . .

Sweat whirls in his mind.
Wayman knows this series of dip and sway
can only be moments before the drop; that these
wobbles of the wing can only lead
to the grating tear of metal
and the tumbling spiral down.
In all seconds of perfect calm
Wayman thinks of the soon and sudden mountain.
A bump could be a stewardess closing a door.
The cabin lights go out.
Lurching, jolting,
Wayman is fainting from fear

or desperately reading somebody
on the nature of death
or statistics on coal.
And though he is probably only a long whine
and a flashing light to you
Wayman is earnestly wanting his terrible aeon to end
— and not *that* way.

Now writing his last words in the sky
Wayman begs as you might peer
up at the lights of a hospital
for you to notice tonight when a plane passes:
consider that Wayman may be aboard.

15

"Yet I continue to fly. I like moving across this continent . . . by whatever means . . . and seeng how people are living their lives.

"Of all the places I've visited, the one that appears most different to me is Quebec. The landscape seems North American, but for me travelling into a different language is like entering another world . . ."

16

Wayman In Quebec

It began simply enough, as an invitation
for Wayman to spend a few days at a lake
in the Laurentians, but as soon as Wayman's car
crossed over the bridge at Hull, what's this?
the trees along the highway suddenly became
"les arbres" and a house
"une maison" and Wayman was relieved to see
the familiar face of Colonel Sanders
revolving reassuringly, but, wait,
below his customary goatee, the Colonel was now selling
"les poulets frits à la Kentucky".

Wayman felt he should be able
after all those high school tests he had endured
to inquire politely as to where he was going:
"Bonjour. Où est la direction à Chénéville?"
or something like that, but his heart sank
at the last moment, and all he could stutter out
was "Chénéville? Chénéville?" *Keep going the way you're headed*
a calm voice comforted him. *Turn left at the next set of lights.*

So he was off through the traffic again
or maybe he was "parmi les autos" or that might be
"les voitures d'occasion" as the signs had it.
Anyway, driving along with "la rivière" gleaming away
behind the riverside farms, that is, "les fermes"
all this time Wayman was considering
How do you say Wayman *in Quebec?* and also
What am I doing here?

17

"In day-to-day life, the automobile is still my main method of transportation. It was a terrible shock when somebody permanently borrowed my car once in Vancouver . . ."

Transport

One morning, Wayman's car is gone. After a minute
Wayman remembers he did drive it back last night
and, yes, left it here in front of the building.
Wayman walks over
and looks at the empty parking space. He bends down
to examine the oil on the asphalt.

Nobody Wayman talks to saw anything suspicious.
Wayman picks up the phone to dial the police
careful to use the number for routine matters.
Missing car? One moment, the police station says.
And then, in a deeper voice: *Police. Emergency.*
"Uh," Wayman says, "I think my car has been stolen."
Well, the voice demands, *has it been stolen*
or hasn't it? "I guess it has," Wayman says.
Okay, the voice says, *in that case I'll fill out a form.*
After giving the details, Wayman asks respectfully
if he should phone back in a day or so
to see if the car has been found.
You can if you like, he is told. *But I wouldn't if I were you.*
If we find it, we'll let you know.

And that was that. In the following days
Wayman resolved more than once to scour the neighbourhood
in case his car had only been taken for a short joyride.
But each time Wayman heads downstairs
intending to get into his machine and go search for it
he realizes again: no car. And a few blocks on foot
teach him he lives in an enormous district.

19

As well, every arrangement to meet some friends at the pub,
each former dash to a movie at the last minute,
now has to be organized: he must leave at a precise instant
in order to be out at the corner on time
to wait for a certain bus.

So, squeezed into the back of a public vehicle
as it lumbers hissing from block to block, moving vaguely downtown,
Wayman starts to dream of the day, months from this, when
after weeks of failing to spot his car out a dusty bus window
and also never discovering it abandoned in any City parking lot,
Wayman can slide behind a strange steering wheel
and begin once more that process
of anxiety, expensive maintenance, and eventual mechanical collapse
which will transform another automobile
— at least for as long as Wayman has it —
into Wayman's car.

"Besides travelling occasionally, through distance like everyone alive I am travelling through time. One gets increasingly aware of this as one gets older . . "

Receding

More every day: Wayman's comb
full of the evidence.
And what Wayman finds scary
is so close to his brain
some things have said
Enough. We've been at this
thirty-five years.
Now we're going to just sit back
and wait for death.

It would be better, Wayman believes,
if the body held a farewell party
for these: if someone made a speech,
presented them with a framed photograph
of how they appeared in 1954,
if their young replacements
attended the gathering out of a sense of duty,
completely bored. Instead,
Wayman learns it has been decided
not only to ignore their departure
but to eliminate these positions.

What if they resent this, Wayman thinks.
What if with so much time on their hands now
they begin to wander around
and try to convince the lungs
or heart
they also have done their share
and ought to stop, sample the good life?
Maybe this is how it happens:
after years of listening to particular follicles
testify to the joys of not working any more
a vital organ agrees
and then some people get quite a shock.
If so, Wayman envies those men
bald rather early
whose stomach at that time probably replied
Quit? Quit?
What for? I enjoy my job.
Perhaps, he reasons, those who go bald while young
live longer?

       Meanwhile,
Wayman is left with his comb,
his forehead growing in the mirror
and the hope the other parts of his body are aware
how soon most people
drop dead after retirement.

BECOMING A CRANK

"I should say a word about how a contemporary poet ordinarily gets poems published. You type up five to ten poems, place them in an envelope, and submit them to the editor of a literary magazine or journal. The editor takes your poems, puts them in a drawer, and six or eight months later pulls them out, rejects them, and mails them back to you.

"So it's a long, depressing procedure getting anything published. After a while, though, you become cunning. Instead of having just one package of poems out, you send off two, three, more. This way, at any time there are hundreds of your poems winging through the mails. You become like a juggler: as soon as one package of poems comes back from a magazine, you quick as a wink whip it out of the old envelope, stick it into a new envelope, and mail it away again.

"The first university teaching job I ever had was in Colorado, where besides my classroom duties I was to be poetry editor of the little magazine they published there. I was very excited about this, because for the first time I was going to be at the other end of this process. I was going to be the one who decided if someone else's poems were published . . ."

Life On The *Land Grant Review*

Mad gnome of an assistant editor
Wayman gloats in Colorado
before the mass of manuscripts now his,
his to edit.

Wayman remembers the mounds of his own mail back
marked: "Are you kidding?"
"What is this grunt?" and
"Do us a favor and stick this up your ass"

Now the tide is turned: all literary America
lies at Wayman's feet; America, with a poet
under every rock. Revenge, revenge,
the very word is like a Bedlam gong
to ring him deeper into rage . . .
"And that's a literary reference,"
Wayman shrieks, slashing someone's poem to
shreddies as he writes rejections
— the same for all: Miss Elsa Eddington Brewster,
editor Riley of the *Southwest Pawnee County Quarterly,*
former associates with their cringing, oily letters.
Only the editor-in-chief's friends
give him pause. Wayman weighs
the first-name-basis missives carefully.
Who is putting him on? Who really studied
under Yvor with the boss? Who knew him when?
Who now? Is everybody faking?

Feverish in the cool Colorado evening
Wayman is hammering away at rejecting
faster and faster. The earth heaves,
the business manager elopes,
the editor is arrested in Utah with the funds,
still Wayman is scribbling: "No." "No."
Imperceptibly the word spreads outward
to those in Portland, Oregon and Portland, Maine
stuffing their packages of poems
into the 10 p.m. mailbox slots:
"Wayman," the news has it,
"Wayman's editing in Colorado.
All we can do is submit."

"A long-standing source of inspiration and ideas for me has been the poems . . . in translation . . . of the Chilean poet Pablo Neruda. I first learned about Neruda from the American poet Robert Bly when I was in California.

"Being influenced in this way by the work of others can be a great help, but it can also be overwhelming . . ."

Influences

I sit down at my desk
— and it turns into Pablo Neruda!
His stout face stares thoughtfully
up from between my pencils.
I say to him: *Please. I want to get on with it.*
On with being Wayman, with my own work.
Vanish. Vamos! And he goes.

But just then my chair feels uncomfortable.
I jump up and look. Neruda again.
Pablo, I tell him. *Please, I insist.*
Leave me alone. I've got to do it.
Back to your Chile. Get south.
Sud! Sud! Leave Vancouver to me.

And he goes. I draw out my papers,
my scribbles. Scratching my beard.
I pore over a fine adjustment,
searching for the perfectly appropriate sound.
Then I notice the curtain
leaning over my shoulder.
"I'd do it this way," it says, pointing.
"Change this word here."

Neruda, I say, getting real mad.
Flake off. Go bother Bly.
Teach all the poets of California.
While I'm talking to him like this
he changes from being my curtains
to a pen. And I see his eyes twinkle
as they fall on my typewriter.

Then, I get cagey.
I'll be back in a minute, I tell him
and leave, carefully shutting him
inside the room.
Out on my porch, in the cold air
I see the North Shore mountains behind the City.
I'm alone now, shivering.
There is no sound over the back yards
but traffic
and a faint Chilean chuckle.

31

"Among the many uncertainties associated with writing and publishing is the question of how your work is received. It is of course very pleasant if editors, publishers, reviewers, and so on say they like what you do. But we know from literary history the judgment of such folk isn't always the most astute.

"Thus, being considered 'successful' by those who currently get to hand out that designation doesn't free you from sharing the same problems that affect everyone . . ."

The Day After Wayman Got The Nobel Prize

The day after Wayman got the Nobel prize
he discovered the problem was still there:
how good are his poems?
The poems that are not particularly staggering, or new
to him, or the one that is a terse masterpiece in the afternoon
and is empty by nine o'clock that night.
Always the clean page and the words, the English words.
And what for?

Not to mention the rent, if no difficulty now
as Wayman unfolds the strange cheque from Sweden
then in a month or so, when the landlord drops by again.
And the car needs plugs and points.
And there is the lovely round body of the beautiful woman
Wayman has never been able to touch.

Like the Monday after the Revolution
when we were told to drive to work as usual
so on the morning after a little success Wayman still
can't help knocking the sugar over as he reaches for coffee.

The day after his acceptance speech was published
and again after his reading in Carnegie Hall
Wayman began to wonder
about the day after death.

"Few authors are ever pleased with their publishers, and I daresay the feeling is mutual. These days I'm grateful if anything imaginative or thoughtful or pleasantly unexpected happens with books of mine. But when I was young and foolish, I thought a good deal more should occur when a book was accepted for publication . . ."

Becoming A Crank

In the clutches of his publishers, Wayman became a crank.
It had to do with Wayman's continually expressed opinions
on who buys poetry and why. It had to do with the publishers
carefully ignoring his obviously lucrative ideas.
There *was* a letter from the Director of Advertising, Promotion, and Publicity
welcoming Wayman as "a great addition to the Spring List"
but that had Wayman's first name wrong.
And at the end, there were disagreements about price,
the size, the format, typeface, interior spacing, cover artwork
and a few miscellaneous corrections
— all of which Wayman lost. Unable to generate any responsive spark
Wayman became the crank.

He knew he was a crank when, at a local sales party
he found he could start in about his complaints
while keeping all his attention on the drinks and food.
He knew he was a crank when, as he began to explain his views
to the firm's regional representative
the latter said: "Oh, here is a bookseller.
He's the person you really should speak to . . ." and vanished.
Wayman was launched into it again
when suddenly the bookseller leaned forward
— a freak no older than Wayman, but with his own store —
and said: "Man, this is interesting. But, wow, am I stoned."

Wayman knew he was beat. Numbly getting his hat and coat
he met the Publisher himself, fresh off his plane from the East.
"I just want to let you know we'll do everything we can for you,"
the Publisher said grandly. "Thank you very much," Wayman said
without a trace of irony in his voice,
"I appreciate that." And walking away with his book
— his poor, hard-bound, high-priced, undersold book —
Wayman heard from behind his Publisher say:
"Please don't mention it. After all, it's our *job*."

"Poems, like everything else made by people, are products of a specific time and place. Changes in that time and place will alter poems, subtly or not so subtly . . ."

Metric Conversion

Looking through his poems one day
Wayman suddenly stops, astonished. Just before a line
about driving 450 miles
a highway sign has been erected: two wooden posts painted green
and a thin metal rectangle which states *724 kilometres.*

Wayman flips ahead. Further on
in front of a mention of 300 pounds
another construction announces *136.36 kilograms.*
This sign is even fresher: the green paint
is still tacky when Wayman pokes it with his finger.

Wayman turns directly to a certain poem he remembers
and, sure enough, before a clause that reads
"the temperature was forty degrees"
two wooden posts, unpainted, are stuck into the ground.
On a piece of metal leaning against them, Wayman sees
4 degrees Celsius. And nearby on the grass
two men are eating lunch
surrounded by their tools, cans of paint, lumber and sawhorses.

"What are you doing here?" Wayman asks. "Eating lunch,"
one of the men replies calmly.
"Listen," Wayman says, "I don't want your signs in my poems."
"Are these your poems?" the man asks, looking up.
"Yes," Wayman says. The two men stare at him, chewing thoughtfully.

"I want you to take your signs down and leave," Wayman resumes
after a pause. "It's all right, this is government,"
the younger of the two says. "In any case," the other man begins,
screwing the cap onto his thermos, "the way I view it is
we're doing you a big favor. Degrees Fahrenheit, ounces, yards
— who is going to remember what they meant in a few years?"
Both men have finished their lunches by now and are standing up.

"I don't want those things in my poems," Wayman persists.
"These terms make our ordinary world seem foreign, when it's not."
"Believe me," the older man says, as he and the other
prepare to hoist the metal signboard into place,
        "someday you'll be glad
we installed these. They might seem strange to you now
but without them pretty soon these poems would appear even stranger."

The two men lift the sign. "So instead of just complaining,"
the older man continues,
"could you reach into that toolbox
and pass us some of those five-centimetre nails?"

"In recent years, certain words have crept into movies, television, even articles in magazines and newspapers. Some people persist in believing these words are 'wrong', or bad for you. Schools, by and large, are one of the last bastions of this idea. And this creates a problem for me when, from time to time, I'm asked to give a reading in a high school. . ."

Travelling Companions

At the bus station in Winnipeg,
buying a ticket for Winkler, Manitoba,
Wayman hears a familiar voice behind him:
"Make that two to Winkler." Wayman turns, and
it's Four Letter Word.
"I told you to stay back at the hotel,"
Wayman says. "I'll only be gone for a day.
It's a high school reading
and they asked me specifically not to bring you."
"Nonsense," Four Letter Word says,
reaching past Wayman to pay his portion of the fares.

"You're not welcome there," Wayman insists,
as he struggles out to the bus
with his suitcase and a big box of books to sell.
"That's not the point," Wayman's companion replies
as they hand their tickets to the driver
and climb up into the vehicle.
"Next you'll be ordered not to read
poems that mention smoking or drinking."

"I don't think you understand," Wayman begins
while the bus threads its way through the five o'clock traffic
and out onto the endless frozen prairie.
"The organizers of this program
asked me not to cause any trouble.
It seems somebody like you was brought into a school last year
and there were complaints all the way to the Minister of Education."

Four Letter Word stares out a window
at the darkening expanse of white snow.
"And you're the guy," he says at last,
"who's always telling people
I'm the one that gives the language its richness and vitality.
Didn't Wordsworth declare
poets should speak in the language of real men and women?"

"But it's a high school," Wayman tries to interject.
"Do you think the kids don't swear?" his friend asks.
"Or their parents? And I didn't want to bring this up,"
he continues, "but you depend on me. You use me for good reasons
and without me your performance will flop."
"No, it won't," Wayman says.
"It will," his companion asserts.
And the two ride through the deep winter night
in an unpleasant silence.

An hour later, they pull into the lights of Winkler
and here's the school librarian
waiting in the cold at the bus stop.
"You must be Wayman," he says
as Wayman steps down. "And is this a friend of yours?"
"I never saw him before in my life," Wayman responds
but his companion is already shaking hands with the librarian.
"So good to be here," he says, picking up Wayman's box of books.
"Now, when do we read?"

WAYMAN IN LOVE

"The first of the Wayman poems, Waiting For Wayman, *expresses a puzzle that began for me when I first went to California and which has bothered me ever since . . ."*

Waiting For Wayman

Wayman is in his chair
waiting for Wayman.
He reads in the quiet room.
He looks up at the door,
back to the book, sighs.

The phone rings.
Wayman reaches for it,
hoping it's Wayman.
"Let it all hang out,"
the voice chuckles.
Click. Wayman goes back to his book,

thinks: "What's reasonable about *that?*
What does hanging out have to do with it?"

The page turns blank.
"That's right, isn't it?" Wayman asks.
"Doesn't Wayman have to come?
It's only rational.
Isn't it?" A voice says:
"Whatcha got on — your mind?"
Laughs. Wayman looks at his bookcase.

"I think about it," Wayman says,
"women or drinking or
messing around.
I don't see what it leads to.
I mean, of course I know, but I don't feel
what they're supposed to do when you get them.
What do you have? I mean
you feel good but then what?
Where does it go, and
what's it to do with me?"

Wayman is waiting for Wayman.
He seems very late.
"I think," he says,
"I should write a poem about this."

"Much has been written on the current state of relationships between men and women. Next is my theoretical poem about this..."

Wayman In Love

At last Wayman gets the girl into bed.
He is locked in one of those embraces
so passionate his left arm is asleep
when suddenly he is bumped in the back.
"Excuse me," a voice mutters, thick with German.
Wayman and the girl sit up astounded
as a furry gentleman in boots and a frock coat
climbs in under the covers.

"My name is Doktor Marx," the intruder announces
settling his neck comfortably on the pillow.
"I'm here to consider for you the cost of a kiss."
He pulls out a notepad. "Let's see now,
we have the price of the mattress, this room must be rented,
your time off work, groceries for two,
medical fees in case of accidents. . . ."

"Look," Wayman says,
"couldn't we do this later?"
The philosopher sighs, and continues: "You are affected too, Miss.
If you are not working, you are going to resent
your dependent position. This will influence
I assure you, your most intimate moments . . . ."

"Doctor, please," Wayman says. "All we want
is to be left alone."
But another beard, more nattily dressed,
is also getting into the bed.
There is a shifting and heaving of bodies
as everyone wriggles out room for themselves.
"I want you to meet a friend from Vienna,"
Marx says. "This is Doktor Freud."

The newcomer straightens his glasses,
peers at Wayman and the girl.
"I can see," he begins,
"that you two have problems . . . ."

"As we grow older, we may feel we understand more about human behavior. But this doesn't seem to make it any easier if suddenly you have to take part again in the rituals our society has developed for getting to know members of the opposite sex . . ."

Wayman In Circulation

After more than two years, Wayman and his girl call it quits.
Wayman reaches for the phone again, delighted, but as he is dialing
an old scar floats to the surface of his psyche like a bubble in hot water:
what will the woman he is about to call think of his squeaky voice?

And in the days that follow, each of Wayman's old anxieties
reappear: how do his armpits smell?
Every terror he was sure he had safely outgrown
he now discovers was off taking classes growing bigger
and meaner and cleverer: did he brush his teeth?
What *is* he supposed to do at her door saying goodnight?

Wayman finds he has stumbled out of all the ease
of a customary relationship
into a new nervous world where he wants to make a good impression.
But he has to pick his nose, even if just for a second.
And if he lets this fart out slowly, perhaps she won't notice it's him?

Two years older, his emotional life
once more transformed into a puddle of apprehension and despair
Wayman is back in circulation.
Despite his frightening interpersonal history, however,
his endless betrayal by his body

Wayman has a date for Saturday night.

ACTIVELY SEEKING EMPLOYMENT

"One interesting part of the working life is being told you're not wanted on a job. The first time it happened to me was at the end of my first year of teaching college, in Colorado. A senior member of the department took me aside to deliver the message . . ."

Getting Fired

for Al Purdy

Wayman, I like you in a way.
I don't agree with you of course
and I'm not sure you belong here.
I was out digging fenceposts yesterday
— you've seen my little spread —
and when I took out the old posts
I found they'd been sunk six feet down:
built to last a hundred years.
Me, I've got an investment in the kids here,
these students. I understand them.
I'm sinking my posts
nine feet down: going to last two hundred years.

I want you to call off these complaints:
petitions and so on, people coming round
all the time to see the chairman,
the deans on the phone to him every day.
He's worked hard to be chairman; I don't want
a nice country boy like him
in trouble over a thing like this.

So if you appeal, we'll have to do what we can.
Actually, I'd like all this business forgotten
and you going with no unpleasantness
or black marks on your record.
I think you should just leave
without all this fuss.
Instead of making trouble
and then us having to take measures in return
why don't you just get the fuck out of Dodge.

"When I returned to Canada in 1969, I worked for a while on a crew doing demolition and construction in a seedy part of Vancouver..."

Wayman In The Workforce: Urban Renewal

Neil, Brian, Jeff, Rick, Mark,
Steve D., Steve W., Swede, Tom,
Richard, Abe, Bill, and Mike, too.

Forty feet over the floor, on a shaking scaffold
Wayman is in the workforce.
After eighteen years of education
Wayman is out cleaning bricks.
But as he peers down from his wall
knuckles white where he grips the guardrail
Wayman sees through the winter dusk
there is something inefficient
about modern industry. He realizes
everybody is drunk.

There are the gyproc-ers. Passing each other nails,
beer and sheetrock, they hammer the boards
onto the framing. And over the windows.
Across the doors. Through the plumbing.

Tapers are working behind them. John Senior
lies sprawled at the foot of a ladder
dreaming of Scotch. Smitty is up on it
sanding, reeling about as his ceiling goes round and round.
Mescalito is mudding the joins, pupils large
in the night. He mutters spells against goodness
taught him long ago in the grotto in San Francisco
the day he was enrolled as a warlock.
"Tabor! Tabor!" he chants, mud in his evil beard.

Dan the Foreman is out
eating supper at Wing's. Wing's menu is brief:
Persian, Siamese or Alley meat stew.
Back at the site, the construction boys
sit at the edge of the loft and drink.
They are cursing the owner
whom no one has seen for days.
Peel the plumber is busy installing
shower heads, that later will be discovered
simply to hang in the wall. Unconnected
to anything. Milo the electrician
tests for current. Two fingers go
in each socket. He gives a slight twitch;
there is the smell of burnt flesh.
He notes the results on a clipboard happily,
stumbling among the empties.

Up from the sidewalk come the howls of the bums.
Tonight they have organized: John the Colonel,
Reggie Wheelchair, Montana and the Leopardskin Coat
are together. "Eight cents.
Eight cents for a starter," they call.

And Wayman hears from his perch. Somehow
someone has passed him a bottle, too.
High over the building trades, Wayman considers his future.
He wonders if they have brick walls
in the breweries.

"For about a year and a half in the early 1970s, I worked as a high school English department marker ... a non-teaching teacher's aide ..."

Wayman In The Workforce: Teacher's Aide

Through the late snows of March, Wayman ploughs into the parking lot
his car sputtering through the slushy drifts.
Wayman is here to spend hours marking
what the students have scrawled off in seconds between the bells:
endless crinkly sheets of Grade 11 English essays.

Only Wayman takes it seriously. Every apostrophe is always misplaced.
Every sentence runs on like a television set. One student writes
he likes to hang around hippies "because they are so down and out
they make me feel positively good." Another compares
a hamburger sauce of ketchup and mayonnaise, oozing out of a bun
to "the wounds of a dying soldier."

Some afternoons nobody comes. The classes
simply take the day off. Wayman stays at his desk in the library
marking, marking. Every so often
he looks up from his piles of paragraphs
and stares at the empty chairs.

He hears a noise in the quiet. Behind him on the library rug
the Director of English 11 sits, in the full lotus.
He is throwing the I-Ching. "When the students are absent
I have a chance to pursue my hobbies," the Director says brightly.
"Did you know that extending the lines of the Star of David
yields the figure of the Maltese Cross?"

Wayman pushes his nose deeper into his papers.
Outside the first green April buds begin, and inside
Wayman begins to sigh. In the spring
his nuts boil over like an old radiator. Day by day
he watches the skirts in the hallway creep slowly up
the 17-year-old fleshy thighs. Breasts seem to swell
under thinner and thinner cotton blouses.
Wayman checks and re-checks his columns of grades.

And on the last day, in June, all the green trees flower.
Wayman turns in his pencils and walks out
past the clock and the picture of the Queen.
He starts his car and drives out of the schoolyard
into the summer. Headed home through the warm afternoon,
    he realizes
he has been marking time.

"But I never gave up applying for jobs teaching college English. . ."

Not Getting Hired

"Writing? This is an *English* department.
Frankly I can't see what use a writer could be."
And also: "Only one book? My friend,
we have literally dozens of applications from poets.
Unless you've done more than this, I'm afraid you'll just go in the pile."

As well, there was a Bursar and Dean of Instruction
who became incensed at Wayman's subversive notions:
"That's how you'd mark an English paper? Do you never use
any other criteria besides your own subjective opinions?
Just answer the question, Mr. Wayman: yes or no."
There was one of a selection committee who invited Wayman
to attend a lecture on Marxist Aesthetics that afternoon.
In the silence that followed Wayman's reply, the Head
leaned forward gravely: "All of us in the Department are going
you know. We'd be very interested
in your reasons for not wishing to attend."

Then there was an appointment for nine p.m., after a long day
dragging boards all around a jobsite. "Enthusiasm, man!"
the Dean of Curriculum and Instruction wanted, as he pounded
one arm of his chair. "Think big. This college is going places.
You'll have to step lively if you want to come along with us."
And there was a university Wayman was keen to impress,
        where he spoke
with great speed and skill about his plans, his hopes, his ideas.
Later, Wayman heard the Chairman had thoughtfully fingered
a small white pamphlet after Wayman left.
"And did you notice his pupils?" the Chairman had asked.
"How large they were? Obviously, the man is on drugs."

Everywhere, the impossible gigantic question:
"Now if you were setting up a basic composition program
how would you go about it?" And: "We find in our classes sometimes
we can utilize other media besides print. How do you feel about this?"
One night, a horrible dream
in which Wayman goes to see Neil at the site
to ask for his old job back, and finds Neil has appointed
a selection committee: Danny, Pat Flynn and John Davies
sit waiting amid the scaffolds and sawdust.
Danny asks the first question: "Now, Wayman,
lately we've been putting our gyproc nails
eight inches apart. What are your thoughts on that?"

Everyone's eyes turn toward him, watching.

"Looking for any kind of work, you have to engage in what the Unemployment Insurance Commission calls 'actively seeking employment' . . . "

Wayman In The Workforce: Actively Seeking Employment

Everybody was very nice. Each place Wayman went
the receptionist said: "Certainly we are hiring.
Just fill out one of these forms." Then, silence.
Wayman would call back each plant and corporation
and his telephone would explain: "Well, you see,
we do our hiring pretty much at random. Our interviewers
draw someone out of the stack of applications we have on file.
There's no telling when you might be notified: could be next week
or the week after that. Or, you might never hear from us at all."

One Thursday afternoon, Wayman's luck ran out.
He had just completed a form for a motor truck
manufacturing establishment, handed it in to the switchboard operator
and was headed happily out. "Just a minute, sir," the girl said.
"Please take a seat over there. Someone will see you about this."

Wayman's heart sank. He heard her dialing Personnel.
"There's a guy here willing to work full time
and he says he'll do anything," she said excitedly.
Around the corner strode a man in a suit. "Want a job, eh?" he said.
He initialled one corner of the application and left.
Then a man in a white coat appeared. "I'm Gerry," the newcomer said.
"This way." And he was gone through a doorway into the plant.

"We make seven trucks a day," Gerry shouted
standing sure-footedly amid a clanking, howling, bustling din.
"Over here is the cab shop, where you'll work. I'll be your foreman.
And here is the chassis assembly . . ." a speeding forklift
        narrowly missed them
". . . and this is where we make the parts."
"Wait a minute," Wayman protested, his voice barely audible
above the roar of hammers, drills, and the rivet guns. "I'm pretty green
at this sort of thing."

        "Nothing to worry about," Gerry said.
"Can you start tomorrow? Monday? Okay,
you enter through this door. I'll meet you here."
They were standing near an office marked *First Aid*.
"We have to do a minor physical on you now," Gerry said.
"Just step inside. I'll see you Monday."

Wayman went shakily in through the First Aid office doors.
"I need your medical history," the attendant said
as Wayman explained who he was. "Stand over here.
Thank you. Now drop your pants."
Wayman did as he was told. "You seem sort of nervous to me,"
the aid man said, as he wrote down notes to himself.
"Me, I'm a bit of an amateur psychologist. There are 500 men
in this plant, and I know 'em all.
Got to, in my job. You shouldn't be nervous.
Remember when you apply for work you're really selling yourself.
Be bold. Where are you placed? Cab shop?
Nothing to worry about working there: monkey see, monkey do."

Then Wayman was pronounced fit, and the aid man escorted him
back through the roaring maze into the calm offices of Personnel.
There Wayman had to sign for time cards, employee number,
      health scheme
and only just managed to decline
company credit union, company insurance plan, and a
      company social club.
At last he was released, and found himself back on the street
clutching his new company parking lot sticker in a light rain.
Even in his slightly dazed condition,
a weekend away from actually starting work, Wayman could tell
he had just been hired.

"I stayed at this truck plant job for about eight months . . ."

The Kenworth Farewell

Everyone wore eyeglasses for safety.
To Wayman at first the factory had the look
of a studious crew of graduate students
dressed by mistake in torn and baggy coveralls
who had wandered in through the high aisles of stacked parts
to stand aimlessly amid the machines and assembly stations.

And the boys in Cab Build
were hooting: *Whoop. Whoop.*

Settling in, getting to know the place, Wayman discovered
both box-end and open-end wrenches, fine- and coarse-threaded nuts.
Also the forklifts, which never failed to release
a warm fart of propane when Wayman passed behind them.
And Wayman meanwhile got real intimate with his wristwatch:
staring at each minute in every hour
until somehow it turned into a morning, and even an entire day.

And the boys in Cab Build
were hooting: *Whoop. Whoop.*

Wayman returned home each late afternoon to the rebirth of a bath:
the grand feel of fresh clothes against his skin.
Picking the dirt out of his nose, he understood
not only was he in the factory, the factory was in him, too.

So he learned all the Kenworth slogans:
"It's only a truck", and "It's only a Kenworth",
and "At sixty miles an hour, who is going to know the difference?"
Also: "There's a right way, a wrong way,
and a Kenworth way." And Wayman mastered
the Great Kenworth Fault Game: "It isn't *my* fault."
Even if an error took only a minute to fix
like forgetting to drill safety light holes, for example,
everyone argued happily for hours
all the cosmic questions and implications
of each other's ultimate innocence and guilt.

Wayman learned the faces, and what each meant.
Working with young Bill was a rain of washers
he and Larry endlessly tossed back and forth.
Wayman discussed women with so many, only to later discover
they were just out of high school and still living at home.

And there was the day Gerry the foreman complained about the quota:
"I have seven hoods to get out today, but what do I have
to do it with? A hunky (meaning Daniluk),
a hippie (meaning Wayman)
and a God damn sky pilot . . ." (meaning Wayne
who before Wayman left finally cornered him
and gave him one pamphlet on the Four Spiritual Laws
and another called — Wayne said: "Don't worry about the title" —
Jesus and the Intellectual.)

And the boys in Cab Build
were hooting: *Whoop. Whoop.*

Wayman might have stayed forever.
But his first clue was a Monday morning
when it seemed the weekend had never occurred.
The second clue was Paul Palmer telling him
(Palmer the mainstay of the Pipe Shop's
Hose Amputation Division):
"I've worked at this bench a year, but it feels as though
I might have been here one day, or always."
And so often the great gleaming $50,000 trucks
wouldn't start at the end of the Final Line
and had to be towed out into the yard — which broke Wayman's heart.
Also there was a moment when Wayman found himself
in his own car rolling down the highway near Bellingham:
heading north again on a Sunday, but driving just the same
on that beautiful concrete freeway which he knows also drifts
south in a dream towards California.

So Wayman at the end picked up his toolbox,
shook hands with the foreman
and walked out another time through the Kenworth Keyhole:
that man-sized door set into a truck-sized door
on which someone has thoughtfully painted "Door".
Wayman passed out of the world of tires and fibreglass dust,
timeclocks, and the long sessions upstairs in the can.

And as the boys in Cab Build
howled their last farewell: Wayman
was on his way once more.

70

"When I finish with a job, I like to go for a drive across North America as a holiday and reward for myself. It often appears to me that when I do this I become another sort of person than I was before . . ."

Wayman Ascending Into The Middle Class

In the middle of a trans-Canada excursion
while he visits for a week with the parents of a friend
Wayman lies in a hammock through the hot August days.
Far behind him now are the horrible winter mornings
he got up in the dark and dragged his lunchbox off to work.
Here, as he sips a drink in the gently rocking couch
scarcely a thought crosses his mind about his old companions
still probably stumbling about complaining as they
hammer nails, steer tugboats
or chase logs through the bush a thousand miles away.

A light breeze springs up. Through half-closed eyes
Wayman contemplates flowers, and a leafy screen.
He begins to sway into sleep. The beer bottle
slips out of his languid grasp
and falls almost silently onto
the thick green lawn. Wayman sighs.
He feels himself float
in his hammock, and begin to drift upwards:
ascending, as he snores
into the middle class.

"In the summer of 1976, I worked in Toronto part-time on a CBC-FM national arts show. The experience for me linked together a number of the crazier aspects of employment, Canadian publishing, and the electronic media. . ."

Wayman On Air

for Peter, Gary, Barb and Anne

The great CBC transmission mast
towers over Jarvis Street.
At its base throb the engines of immense generators
and gigantic air-conditioning intakes.
Beside these, the mobile studios
and the portable earth station for Canada's communication satellites
are parked amid the Corporation's fleet of cars and trucks.
Nearby in the huge underground room of Master Control
calm-eyed technicians sip coffee
as they watch the banks of flickering lights and gauges.
Now one cooly pushes a sequence of buttons
to adjust a live feed from Ottawa.
Another is tuning a series of knobs to ensure
the sound reaching Calgary is exactly perfect.

A floor above, in the Radio building,
through the thick pane of soundproof glass
in Broadcast Studio H, all the power and technology
of an entire national communications network
is focussed for this instant on a single microphone.
And behind it
sits Wayman, babbling nervously
about *poems.*

75

The host of the program, Peter, is looking at Wayman incredulously.
Poets are the bane of the host's life anyway:
the ones who are reasonably articulate on the phone
and then freeze up in the studio,
the ones who take offense at the simplest question
and then stay in a huff for the rest of the interview
and those who, six months after Peter's last show was cancelled,
still pursue him to appear on it.

                         Yet Wayman
keeps talking. All summer he has been presenting the host
with twenty minutes of recorded interviews with poets
once each week. And just like the producer told him,
on air he has been desperately dredging up anecdotes
in the hope of enlivening his recorded material.
Wayman notices, though,
a gleam of interest in Peter's eyes
only when Wayman, then a number of his guests,
mention that a book of poems in Canada usually sells a thousand copies.
"Just a thousand?" Peter inquires,
with a tone in his deep FM voice that suggests
these people are not merely unsavory,
they are also less than worthy of airtime. It was then Wayman decided
— during the only moments of his life
when every one of his words was carried coast-to-coast faster than thought —
there are some things
better left unsaid.

Wayman On Air: 2. Interviewing

During the tapings, Wayman would sit politely
sweating while his interviewee
rambled on happily far off the topic.
Behind his guest, through the glass
Wayman could see Lorne, the technician, in the control booth
carefully examining his fingernails
while beside him Gary, the studio director,
scribbled advice frantically on little white cards
held up for Wayman to read: *Ask what he means by that*
or *Confusing!*
and once when things were going especially badly —
a single, despairing, wiggly line.

So Wayman would frown intently
keeping one eye on the time, one eye
on Gary's messages, and any spare eye
fixed interestedly on his guest:
"Gee. That's fascinating. Could you elaborate on that?"
At which the guest's voice would falter,
his face would close,
and under Lorne's skilled fingers the sensitive pick-up heads
of the expensive tape recorders
would dutifully begin preserving
the tick of the studio clock.

Wayman arranged a session with a noted professor,
but as soon as the professor started to respond
to Wayman's opening comments
it was all Wayman could do to insert an intelligent grunt
into the professor's erudite, effortless flow of ideas.
After Wayman managed to break in
clumsily a couple of times
he realized his most immediate statement
was the opposite of what he had said last.
"That's all right," the professor said generously,
dismissing Wayman's fumbled explanation with a wave,
"we all contradict ourselves." And he was off again.

Wayman interviewed Jewinski,
Toronto's poet-policeman,
and thought he had done an excellent job
of sympathetically eliciting accounts of life on the force.
But later Wayman was told by a mutual friend
Jewinski wasn't so sure. "I could see,"
Jewinski had reported, "Wayman was nervous.
And if there's one thing I know from my job:
if someone is nervous,
they're guilty."

And so it went, week by week:
Wayman would stumble from the studio
dizzy with effort, satisfied only
he had wrung everything possible
out of either his subject or himself.
In the hall would be Gary
jauntily flourishing the tape.
"And now," Gary would say,
as he beckoned Wayman to follow him toward the editing room,
"we're ready to start *work*."

Wayman On Air: 3. Editing

After each interview, Gary would feed the tape
into the editing machine, shaking his head,
and would promptly run whatever marvellous moments of sparkle and wit
or literary-historical importance Wayman *had* managed to capture
straight onto the floor. "We have to clear the junk away first,"
Gary would say, as Wayman watched horrified,
". . . meanwhile, would you hand me my coffee?" Little by little
Gary reassembled what was left of the session, though:
taking a coherent thought from the first few minutes
and splicing it beside a moment or two of lucidity
that had appeared twenty minutes later.
On the thin, heavily-scarred piece of vinyl
Wayman's voice began to emerge
as though he was a master of succinct questions
and his guest as though he knew precisely what he was talking about.
As a grand finale Gary would remove all Wayman's false starts,
his stutters, and most of the "um"s. But even when the tapes
were edited to Gary's grudging acceptance
Wayman learned they were subject to shelf disease:
a sickness Wayman first thought
might turn any prerecorded tape brownish-green and slimy in its box
like a head of lettuce left too long in the refrigerator.
Yet it was just that a tape considered eminently playable one day
was generally understood to sound terrible
when it was ready to be aired a few days later.

But they got used anyhow.
Despite everything, each week
Wayman would find himself outside the control room
about to go into the studio to sit with the host
and surround his tape with a live bubble of talk.
Through the door he could see Lorne at the console
busy checking and refining the input, alert at any second
to take the word from Joanne, the production assistant,
to activate any of the discs and tapes
previously threaded and cued for the day's show.

And Wayman's effort was there among them.
Suddenly Gary would shoot back in his swivel chair
and nod at Wayman
who, clutching his briefcase full of notes,
would bound past the thirty-seven musicians
standing around the hallway waiting their turn.
As the light above the studio door changed
momentarily from red to green,
Wayman stepped through to the room that would once more take him
into the air.

"I received an appointment to teach English again from a university located in downtown Detroit. People I know in Canada would ask me if this job wasn't dangerous . . ."

The Detroit State Poems: Security

Across the campus, small blue lights
mark the location of help telephones.
At building entrances, on each floor of the parking structures,
even along the sidewalks of the adjoining business district
the lights burn above small metal boxes
that contain phones to connect the user
with the university police.
After dark, so many blue lights are visible
the scene looks like an airfield landing strip by night.

Yet Wayman was puzzled
why the phones are not linked
directly to the authorities: a five-digit number
(prominently stenciled on the boxes)
must be dialed first. Perhaps, Wayman reasoned,
the idea is to grasp the phone in one hand,
dial with the other
and fend off any attacker with one foot?
But when he practised this at home, Wayman had to conclude
the best thing for him under these circumstances
would be to rip the receiver out of the box
and as quickly as possible knock himself unconscious with it.

Nevertheless, day and night
the university's patrol cars
vigilantly cruise the region.
And there is constant routine surveillance
by City Police vehicles from a precinct station nearby.
As well, three cameras
mounted atop different buildings
continuously scan potential trouble spots.
And the university's chief of security services
is always willing to unroll the statistics
which prove the campus to be as safe as the most distant suburb.

Naturally, though, incidents do happen.
The summer before Wayman went to work there,
a student was walking with his girlfriend and her child
when another stroller suddenly produced a gun
and demanded money.
                    "No," the student said,
so the other man shot and killed him
and took his wallet with a little more than three dollars in it.

Wayman would refer to this event in his classes,
intending to demonstrate the concept of values.
"I'd give him the cash," Wayman would say.
"I can always get more money but I only have one life.
In fact, if it was me," Wayman went on quickly
as he noticed some of his larger and more surly students
beginning to pay close attention,
"I'd give credit cards, my watch, even post-dated cheques."

Wayman's classes didn't agree. "It's a matter of principle,"
one young woman said, as the others nodded.
"If you start by giving in
who knows where it would end?"
"But it's your *life*," Wayman pleaded.
"Nope," the young woman objected firmly.
"You have to stand up
for what you believe."

                    "You can't stand
if you're full of lead," Wayman retorted,
and the dispute continued until the bell.
And afterwards, as usual,
Wayman got in his car and returned across the river
to the small, safe, Ontario town where he lived
while his students, still convinced of their side of the question,
went back to the residence halls on campus
or drove home even deeper into Detroit.

"Because of what I have seen and experienced in my life, I remain convinced the human race can create a better method of organizing society than the examples currently available on the planet . . ."

Meeting Needs

I walk into the Waldorf bar on Hastings one evening
in case Mark, or anybody I know, is here
and at a couple of tables pushed together
a group of men and women appear familiar.
"Wayman," one of the men calls,
waving me over,
but I can't place where I've seen him before.
"Sit down, sit down," he says enthusiastically.
"We were just talking about you."

As I sit, somebody puts a beer in front of me
and I fumble to add my money to the pile.
"We figured you'd be down tonight,"
the man continues, and around the tables
other heads nod agreement.
"It's, uh, great to see you," I say,
taking a sip of my beer. "But —
where do I know you from?"
"Don't you recognize us?" asks a voice from the other table,
and I realize everyone is staring at me now:
"We're your needs."

"My needs?" I say,
putting down my beer glass. There are about ten of them,
young, casually dressed, as though just off work.
Of the two women present, I can't help observing
how beautiful one is, and to my surprise
she smiles back.

"Certainly,"
the man who first spoke to me says.
"I'm Friendship. This pig beside me,"
he gestures to a portly young man in a windbreaker
with his mouth full of potato chips, "is Food."
"You really don't remember us?" the young man on my left breaks in,
and I notice he has a carpenter's apron, hammer, and hard hat
on the floor by his chair. "That's Shelter,"
Friendship resumes, "and the dude past him in the fancy cowboy shirt
is Clothing."

      "Pleased to meet you,"
I say, extending my hand. "We first met when you were a baby,"
Clothing says as we shake,
"but you probably don't recall that."
"No," I say, and Friendship goes on with the introductions.
By now I can grasp what's happening,
and assume accurately that the one half-slumped
at the other end of the table is Drink
and wait impatiently for Friendship to get around
to the particularly lovely woman, who, sure enough,
smiles invitingly at me once more.
When Friendship finishes, I try to broach a delicate question:
"If you're my needs," I inquire,
"shouldn't there be someone here named, uh,
New Stereo?" "Only you can answer that,"
Friendship says, looking at me intently:
"We're your needs, not your wants."
While I'm considering this,
Food stands up
and asks if anyone would like more beer nuts or anything.
"Naw, but get us another round,"
Drink requests, and I turn to Friendship again.
"There's somebody missing who I think *is* a need of mine,"
I say: "Where's Major Social Change?"
"The Major?" Shelter responds: "She's . . .
sort of different." "She?" I ask.
"Yeah," two or three people confirm.
"But he's, that is, she's a need we all have," I insist.
"Isn't she one of you?"

88

"Not exactly,"
the beautiful woman down the table says.
"But couldn't we be doing a lot better?" I ask her.
"Shouldn't there be more of you here?
Where's Employment, for instance?"
"He ain't talking to you right now,"
Art, the other woman present, answers.
"You're telling me," I begin,
but we pause for a moment while a waiter
unloads two fresh beer for each of us
and Food returns with a half-dozen packages
of nuts and chips for each table.
"If Employment were here," I resume,
"I have a few thousand complaints
to speak to him about."

                    "He claims you don't like him,"
Friendship says. "The way things are," I explain,
"I don't like what he does when I'm with him
and I don't like what he does to my friends.
I know he's only a reflection of the system we live under . . ."
"Actually, it's the other way around,"
interrupts a small guy with glasses sitting opposite me
I hadn't noticed before.

                    "Okay," I agree, "but my point is
he's not going to improve without Major Social Change.
In fact, without her,
none of you are going to alter much for the better.
Not that you're not adequate now,"
I add hastily, as everyone starts to frown,
"or I guess you wouldn't be here.
But there are others absent too.
Who's responsible for me having a real voice
in what happens to my neighborhood, or the City, or . . .?"

"You mean Self-Determination," Friendship says.
"Whatever he's called," I say.

                                    "She,"
someone corrects from along the table.
"She," I say. "But I'd like her
to be together with Employment."
"She'd put him through some changes,"
Art nods. "Plus," I say,
"there are those of you who haven't met people I know
in quite a while, or who offer a pretty meagre appearance
when you do arrive."
"I'm aware of that," Friendship says.
"And what about me needing to feel confident
some of you aren't going to give me the brush-off
in a month or so?" I go on. "You're talking about Security,"
Shelter says. "Exactly," I say, "which is yet another reason
I'd expect Major Social Change to be with you."

"You've misunderstood something," the little guy with glasses
breaks in again. "The Major always declares her role
is to help us get together with people.
But she maintains when she spent time with us in the past
it didn't work out very well."
"She says something about
a confusion
between means and ends," Shelter says.
"We've been close for years," the little guy resumes,
"but she really isn't one of us.
For example," he continues,
"you'll never find her down here."

"That's her loss," Drink says,
as he beckons the waiter.
And we order the same again all around.

90

"To sum up, then . . ."

Dead End

Feeling morbid in the Spring, Wayman figures
it's time to get ready. He pours himself another coffee
pads over to his desk and begins.
If I should die, think only this of me:
There is some corner of a field somewhere
That is forever Wayman . . . It strikes him suddenly
this has been done. He tries again.
The laws of probability tell us
that every breath we take contains some molecules
from the last gasp of Julius Caesar. Think about that.
At this very moment you may be breathing
some of Wayman's too . . . .

This seems awfully long-winded. Wayman recalls a friend
who refused to read anything longer than a page.
And a newspaper editor who howled at him:
"If you can't say it in a paragraph, forget it."
Remember me this way, Wayman decides:

Say of Wayman's end, as he said himself
of so many unfortunate things that happened to him while he lived:
At least
he got a poem out of it.

WAYMAN

At least he got a poem out of it.

Afterword

Distance From The "I": How The Wayman Poems Began

In the late 1960s, I went down from Vancouver to southern California to study writing at the University of California at Irvine. A number of my friends there were former students of the poet Philip Levine, who taught at the California State University of Fresno. So one day I was shown a fascinating poem by Levine called "Looking For Levine".

The poem is a serious one about Levine's search for his Moroccan-Jewish ancestors, and includes a resonant appraisal of the differences between North African village life and Levine's daily existence in a Fresno suburb. One of the things that struck me about the poem is the effect created by Levine's technique of referring to himself in the third person. The poet as well as the reader appears to be able to observe the central figure in the poem (Levine himself) as though with an impartial, objective eye.

Yet there also seemed to me a large potential for comedy in this idea of a writer examining his life as if from a distance, as though he is only a disinterested spectator. Levine didn't seem aware of this possibility, and to my knowledge he has never again used this technique. But since at that time I was wrestling with various personal problems brought on by the culture clash between Vancouver and southern California, I sat down to try to explore some of my own difficulties using Levine's technique. The result was the first Wayman poem, "Waiting For Wayman".

I don't think Levine's poem is the whole story behind my subsequent adoption of this poetic strategy for a number of other poems, however. After all, your friends seem to know you by your last name — certainly this is how they refer to you in your absence. And just to keep life as complicated as possible, to my friends my brother is known as "Wayman's brother" but to my brother's friends I am known as "Wayman's brother". The confusion evident here, I believe, demonstrates once more a certain potential for humor.

In addition, somewhere in the genesis of the Wayman poems is surely an old campfire tune we used to sing in Boy Scouts, "I Ain't A-Gonna Grieve My Lord No More". Besides the established verses to this ditty, people at a sing-song often would make up lyrics relating to the various misfortunes and failings of others seated right there around the circle. Such a verse might go like this:

> (solo) Oh, you can't get to Heaven . . .
> (chorus) No, you can't get to Heaven . . .
> (solo) In Wayman's car . . .
> (chorus) In Wayman's car . . .
> (solo) 'Cause Wayman's car . . .
> (chorus) 'Cause Wayman's car . . .
> (solo) Won't go that far!
> (chorus) Won't go that far!
> (all) No, you can't get to Heaven
>   In Wayman's car,
>   'Cause Wayman's car
>   Won't go that far!
>   I ain't a-gonna g-r-i-e-v-e
>   My Lord no more!

After this it might be my turn to explain why one couldn't attain eternal bliss via "Ridsdale's boat", and so on into the night.

Whatever origin the Wayman poems ultimately have, though, their most useful aspect to me remains the distancing effect I first noticed in the Levine poem. I feel there is something rather egocentric in any artist presuming to tell an audience how life appears to him or her. This ego is often more noticeable in poetry than in the other arts. The author of a poem doesn't have the space, say, a fiction writer has to construct characters or situations that will embody and/or present the author's conclusions about the human condition. In poetry an audience frequently will get the ego served raw: so many poems filled with "I", "I", "I". Naturally, I write this sort of poem, too, but the Wayman persona lets me present some events and my conclusions about them with more apparently-objective distance than I could if I was writing solely from the viewpoint of the pervasive "I". My hope is that the Wayman persona will give people room to laugh at this blast of ego which, explicitly or implicitly, is a necessary part of every poem in which someone is telling you how he or she is responding to the world.

I should add that the Wayman persona is not me, any more than any character in a poem or story is a real three-dimensional human being. He is simply a character who happens to share my last name and some of my feelings toward certain experiences we both have managed to live through.

Tom Wayman
Nelson, B.C.
Spring 1981

Tom Wayman awarded himself the Nobel Prize for Literature in a poem, "The Day After Wayman Got The Nobel Prize", published in 1974 in his second collection of poetry, *For And Against The Moon: Blues, Yells, And Chuckles*.

"At the time I couldn't stand the suspense of not knowing whether my writing would ever achieve that kind of recognition," Wayman says. "Having received the Prize, I've been free to concentrate solely on producing the very best poems I can."

Events like these are typical of what happens in the poems Tom Wayman writes which feature his character named "Wayman". There are Wayman poems scattered through all five of Tom Wayman's collections of verse published to date, and *The Nobel Prize Acceptance Speech* gathers together the best of these plus seven recent Wayman poems which have never before appeared in book form.

THISTLEDOWN BOOKS

WIND SONGS by Glen Sorestad
DARK HONEY by Ronald Marken
INSIDE IS THE SKY by Lorna Uher
OCTOMI by Andrew Suknaski
SUMMER'S BRIGHT BLOOD by William Latta
PRAIRIE PUB POEMS by Glen Sorestad
PORTRAITS by Lala Koehn
HAILSTORM by Peter Christensen
BETWEEN THE LINES by Stephen Scriver
GATHERING FIRE by Helen Hawley
TOWARDS A NEW COMPASS by Lorne Daniel
NOW IS A FAR COUNTRY by John V. Hicks
OLD WIVES LAKE by J.D. Fry
THE CURRIED CHICKEN APOCALYPSE by Michael Cullen
ANCESTRAL DANCES by Glen Sorestad
EAST OF MYLOONA by Andrew Suknaski
BLUE SUNRISE by Bert Almon
THE MUSHROOM JAR by Nancy Senior
WINTER YOUR SLEEP by John V. Hicks
DIRT HILLS MIRAGE by Barbara Sapergia
LAND OF THE PEACE by Leona Gom
RIG TALK by Peter Christensen
DISTURBANCES by Greg Simison
THE BOOK OF THIRTEEN by Gertrude Story
THE LIFE OF RYLEY by Monty Reid
THE NOBEL PRIZE ACCEPTANCE SPEECH by Tom Wayman